IMAGES
of America

CEDAR POINT

IMAGES
of America

CEDAR POINT

David W. and Diane DeMali Francis

ARCADIA
PUBLISHING

Published by Arcadia Publishing
Charleston, South Carolina

Library of Congress Catalog Card Number: 2003115617

For all general information contact Arcadia Publishing at:
Telephone 843-853-2070
Fax 843-853-0044
E-mail sales@arcadiapublishing.com
For customer service and orders:
Toll-Free 1-888-313-2665

Visit us on the Internet at www.arcadiapublishing.com

CONTENTS

INTRODUCTION

From its rustic beginnings in 1870, Cedar Point has grown into the world's largest amusement park and the "Roller Coaster Capital of the World." Featuring 16 magnificent roller coasters and a grand total of 68 exciting rides, Cedar Point entertains well over 3,000,000 people each summer. Situated on a 364-acre peninsula that separates Lake Erie from Sandusky Bay, Cedar Point is more than an amusement park. It's also a popular family resort that offers overnight guests a choice of four hotels with nearly 1500 rooms and suites. Additional resort accommodations include 224 campground sites, 60 cottages and cabins, 59 RV campsites, and a 665-dock marina. Justifiably, this fabulous facility is regularly voted "Best Amusement Park in the World."

But, such success doesn't happen overnight. In fact, it took more than 130 years for Cedar Point to become the most impressive amusement park ever. In 1870, Louis Zistel traversed Sandusky Bay in his small steamship, taking passengers from Sandusky to the overgrown peninsula known as Cedar Point. Once there, his guests could select from a few primitive resort activities such as quenching one's thirst at a small beer garden or strolling along the beautiful sandy beach. For the next 10 years, the infant resort grew very slowly. Bathhouses were constructed, and various other improvements were made, but it wasn't until the Cedar Point Pleasure Resort Company was organized in 1887 that the little facility began to flourish. The new company was aggressive in its efforts to make the resort profitable. The Grand Pavilion, which still stands today, was built in 1888 and housed a massive theatre, bowling alleys, a photographic studio, a kitchen, cold storage lockers, and offices. In 1892, just a few years after the Grand Pavilion debuted, the resort installed its very first switchback railway roller coaster. Thanks to these additions and other improvements, Cedar Point prospered for just a few years until an economic depression coupled with increasing competition threatened its future.

Fortunately for Cedar Point, an Indiana businessman by the name of George Arthur Boeckling arrived in Sandusky, Ohio late in 1897. Bold, innovative, and tireless, Boeckling formed the Cedar Point Pleasure Resort Company of Indiana (later, the G.A. Boeckling Company) and purchased Cedar Point for $256,000. At last, a successful future for Cedar Point was assured. Until his death in 1931, Boeckling steered Cedar Point on a course that carried it to national prominence. In 1899, he built the resort's first hotel, the Bay Shore. Soon, other hotels appeared around the point: The White House in 1901, the magnificent Breakers Hotel in 1905, and the Cedars in 1915. Boeckling's vision had no boundaries. He created the Cedar Point lagoons, constructed a large theatre, and hired the finest chefs to prepare first class cuisine in the restaurants. In 1907, he initiated passenger steamship service from Cleveland to the Point, and similar service from Detroit and Toledo soon followed. It was Boeckling who transformed the resort into a self-sufficient city complete with its own dairy, bakery, soft drink plant, electric power generating works, sewer and water systems, huge warehouses and coolers, narrow-gauge service railroad, and fire department.

It's not surprising that Cedar Point became a major resort destination and the site of dozens of regional and national conventions. Within a few years, attendance exceeded 1,000,000 people each season, and George Boeckling became a very wealthy man. Although he thought amusement parks were common and not on the same level with his resort, Boeckling could not deny the profits to be made from rides and games. In 1906, he constructed an Amusement Circle at his facility, and forever after, Cedar Point would be known as an amusement park.

The 1920s were, for the most part, prosperous for the resort. A major addition to the Breakers Hotel was constructed, but Boeckling suspected that the business boom would not last and privately warned friends that economic collapse was ahead. Accordingly, he wisely shelved plans for a huge new hotel, a bridge connecting Cedar Point to the mainland, and other improvements. Fortunately, however, he forged ahead with plans for the notorious Cyclone, and the new roller coaster opened on schedule for the 1929 season.

Still making plans for his resort, George Boeckling died on July 24, 1931 at the age of 69. The park made a profit that season, but 17 losing summers followed. Faced with the Depression of the 1930s, followed by the material shortages and travel restrictions of World War II, Cedar Point began to decline. By 1949, it seemed clear that the park would probably not open the following season. Two of the park's three roller coasters had been razed, paint was peeling from buildings, and even the grand Breakers Hotel appeared worn and tired.

But, salvation for Cedar Point came yet again in 1950. That year the park was leased to T.C. Melrose, a prominent hotel operator. Melrose quickly lost interest in Cedar Point, but in 1951, one of his executives, Daniel Schneider, took over the remaining nine years of the original 10-year lease. Although Schneider had little capital, he was determined to renovate the shabby facility. Buildings were painted a bright orange so that visitors couldn't help but notice that improvements were underway. A new Kiddieland was added, and many additions were made to the midway. The old passenger steamship, G.A. *Boeckling,* was retired and replaced with new steel ferries. Schneider's efforts began to bear fruit. After much painting and cleaning, the old Breakers Hotel generated $266,000 in revenues for the 1955 season. Perhaps most importantly, the new Causeway connecting the Cedar Point peninsula with Sandusky was completed in 1957.

Schneider's days at Cedar Point, however, were numbered. A Toledo bond dealer, George A. Roose, became interested in the peninsula and envisioned turning it into an upscale residential community. By February of 1957, Roose and a group of investors had acquired control of the G.A. Boeckling Company. Luckily, the State of Ohio intervened and declared that Cedar Point must remain a recreational venue or become a State Park. Roose and his partners abandoned plans for a residential development and instead, beginning with the 1959 season, initiated a program of expansion and investment that quickly positioned Cedar Point as one of America's leading amusement parks. During the first season under Roose's supervision, attendance rose to 970,000 (as compared to 760,000 during Schneider's last season). By 1963, the park was entertaining 1,500,000 in a season, and that figure rose to 2,555,000 in 1967. Working with a foundation laid by Roose and his associates, Richard Kinzel assumed direction of Cedar Point in 1986. Under Kinzel's brilliant leadership, Cedar Point became the world's largest amusement park and the Roller Coaster Capital of the World. The park's parent company, Cedar Fair Limited Partnership, continues the tradition of expansion by acquiring numerous other amusement parks and water parks throughout the United States.

For the complete history of Cedar Point, see David W. Francis and Diane DeMali Francis', *Cedar Point: The Queen of American Watering Places.*

The authors wish to express their gratitude for the continued support and encouragement from Cedar Point's management team. In particular, we wish to thank John Hildebrandt, Vice President of Marketing; Robin Innes, Director of Public Relations; and Dan Feicht, Media Services Manager. Each shares our love of Cedar Point's colorful and vibrant history. We also wish to thank Larry Wasserman and Robert J. Lindsay for making a collection of wonderful 1950s photos available to us for use in this book.

One

CEDAR POINT'S
EARLIEST SEASONS
1870–1904

Cedar Point, situated on a seven and three-quarter mile long peninsula, separates Lake Erie from Sandusky Bay. Named for the huge number of Cedar trees that are indigenous to the area, Cedar Point at first attracted only hunters and fishermen. (Cedar Point Archives.)

When Cedar Point opened as a recreational attraction in 1870, the peninsula was totally undeveloped and offered few entertainments. Picnicking in the tall grass and underbrush was popular with the ladies, but husbands and fathers were probably enjoying a mug of Sandusky-brewed beer in the beer garden.

In its early days, beautiful, clean sand was Cedar Point's greatest asset. Long before roller coasters and carousels invaded the peninsula, children hid from the summer sun under straw hats while they played.

Most of Cedar Point was covered with sand, which made walking difficult. The early resort operators constructed narrow boardwalks across the peninsula and along the lake in order to make visits more enjoyable. Over many seasons, these wooden walks were widened and illuminated for nighttime strolls.

Because many visitors were German-Americans living in Sandusky, Cedar Point's operators always served German-style beers and wines from local companies. This early beer garden featured a cellar to keep beer kegs and wine bottles cool.

Charles Baetz became part owner of the Cedar Point Pleasure Resort Co. and general manager of the resort for the 1888 season. A beer bottler, cigar and tobacco merchant, and opera house manager, Baetz was also an excellent musician and director of the Great Western Band. (Cedar Point Archives.)

Founded by Baetz in 1867, the Great Western Band provided both concert and dance music at Cedar Point in the 1880s and 1890s. For 50 years, Cedar Point presented daily band concerts, and bandmasters composed a number of marches in honor of the summer resort. (Cedar Point Archives.)

Until 1914, Cedar Point was accessible only via the ferry route from Sandusky to the bay dock. The steamer *R.B. Hayes* was placed on the Cedar Point route in 1882 and was not retired until the First World War. During most of her career, the *Hayes* shared duties with the *A. Wehrle Jr.*

The crew of the *R.B. Hayes* poses for a photo. Seated at the front is the ship's cook, who fed a crew that worked seven days a week during the summer and sometimes endured 18-hour days. The crews of most Cedar Point ships lived onboard during the operating season.

Resort visitors of the 1880s enjoyed the calm summer days on Sandusky Bay. Although some trees had been cut down, Cedar Point was still largely woods and underbrush. This photo was taken near the bay steamship dock, where the marina is now located.

Constructed for the 1888 season, the Grand Pavilion was the first major building erected at Cedar Point. The cavernous structure held a theatre, bowling alleys, a photo studio, a saloon, a kitchen, and cold storage lockers. It was illuminated by 24 gas chandeliers. The gas was generated at a plant that was located a safe distance from the pavilion. (Cedar Point Archives.)

The main hall of the 110-foot-by-168-foot Grand Pavilion featured a large theatre with balcony seating for overflow crowds. The stage could comfortably seat a 60- piece concert band or a complete theatrical or operetta company. Lake breezes kept the hall reasonably comfortable on summer days. (Cedar Point Archives.)

Fraternal organization outings comprised a significant portion of Cedar Point's business during the 1890s and early 1900s. Surrounded by uniformed members of a fraternal group, the Philharmonic Band of Reading, Pennsylvania, poses at the Grand Pavilion.

Manager Baetz constructed an outdoor bandstand between the Grand Pavilion and the beach. Large wooden platforms were placed in front of the bandstand so that spectators would not be required to stand in the deep sand.

Sheltering wings were added to the bandstand to protect visitors from the sun and the rain. Later, the entire bandstand structure was converted into a picnic pavilion, and concerts were moved to a new location.

CEDAR POINT BAY LANDING
1888

By the late 1880s, the bay pier was a substantial structure, and a number of buildings had been erected near the end of the pier. To the right, a campground was established that was particularly popular with Ohio militia and National Guard regiments. (Cedar Point Archives.)

Along the beachside esplanade, and near the Grand Pavilion, the Ladies Pavilion served non-alcoholic beverages to women and children. Here, ladies enjoyed a soda water bar, as well as cakes, fruits, ice cream, lemonade, and other "soft" drinks.

The beach was not as broad as it would become in later years, but it was still one of the resort's leading attractions. The boardwalk, with strings of electric lights for nighttime use, provided an excellent view of swimmers frolicking in the waves. (Cedar Point Archives.)

CEDAR POINT BEACH
1888

The beachfront of the late 1880s featured the bandstand, a pony track, a small refreshment stand, and the resort's first large bathhouse. Off shore is a water trapeze for more daring bathers. The arc lamps cast a bright light and burned with an ominous "sizzling" sound. (Cedar Point Archives.)

18

Like other lakeside resorts, Cedar Point was quick to install a water toboggan during the 1890s. Similar to the more complex Shoot-the-Chutes amusement ride, the water toboggan thrilled patrons with a fast slide down an incline and into the lake. (Cedar Point Archives.)

In 1892, Cedar Point's first roller coaster, the Switchback Railway, was built near the beach. Designed by L.A. Thompson, the inventor of the roller coaster, it was installed just eight years after the first pleasure railway debuted at Coney Island.

George Arthur Boeckling (1862–1931) arrived at Cedar Point in 1897, and the next season began his amazing transformation of the resort. He steered a failing little resort along a course to national prominence and was, for many years, "The King of Cedar Point." (Cedar Point Archives.)

One of Boeckling's first goals was to establish Cedar Point as a full-scale resort with overnight accommodations. The Bay Shore Hotel (extreme right) opened in 1899, while the larger White House Hotel opened two years later. The White House had 55 rooms and was equipped with electric lights, call bells, and wide verandas.

Beginning in 1899, Boeckling started publishing brochures that were widely distributed to promote the resort. As the resort grew, the brochures became larger, more attractive, and very colorful.

Boeckling was tireless in his efforts to attract large conventions to Cedar Point. Many booked the resort for an entire week. Each group identified its members and guests with elaborate ribbons, medals, or pinbacks.

Cedar Point's second roller coaster, the Figure 8 Roller Toboggan, debuted amid much excitement for the 1902 season. Although tame by later coaster standards, the Figure 8 nonetheless provided a thrilling ride in its day. (Cedar Point Archives.)

In 1903, Boeckling leased a small plot of land to the Ohio State University. The Lake Laboratory was quickly established and conducted biological research on the lake and the shore. After several years, the spreading resort began to encroach on the laboratory. Eventually, in 1918, Ohio State University moved its facility to Put-In-Bay.

August Kuebeler Jr. was one of George Boeckling's most trusted lieutenants. The son of a Sandusky beer magnate, Kuebeler was appointed vice president of the Cedar Point Pleasure Resort Co. (Glenn Kuebeler Collection.)

Built in 1904, the Crystal Rock Castle was devoted exclusively to serving beer in large glass mugs. It was named for Crystal Rock Beer, the beloved local brand of the Kuebeler-Stang Brewing Co. of Sandusky. (Cedar Point Archives.)

23

Harry Ward became known as "The Grand Old Man of Cedar Point." Ward was hired by Boeckling in 1898, and by 1911, was manager of the new bathhouse. Eventually settling in the maintenance department, Ward did not retire until 1962.

Under the supervision of the tireless Boeckling, Cedar Point was active throughout the year. Caretakers, headed by Boeckling's brother August, lived on the peninsula all winter, but construction workers made the daily trip across the frozen bay by sled.

Even before Cedar Point developed an amusement area, there were a few rides scattered about the grounds. In addition to a roller coaster and carousel, there was a diminutive steam railroad. Owned by Heine Gross, the 4-4-0 engine "Hattie" was a favorite of the children. (Cedar Point Archives.)

During the early 1900s, Boeckling continued to improve Cedar Point by planting grass, flowers, shrubs, and trees. The Grand Pavilion was fully renovated, and Boeckling established very high standards for the cuisine served in the building's dining room.

Tables were placed under trees that still covered much of the resort, and a pleasant picnic ground was created not far from the main resort area. In order to stimulate beer and soft drink sales, however, drinking water was kept in short supply in the picnic grove. (Cedar Point Archives.)

A monument saluting Civil War veterans was erected overlooking the beach. A shrewd businessman and brilliant publicist, Boeckling recognized that veteran groups like the Grand Army of the Republic were a lucrative source of revenue for the resort.

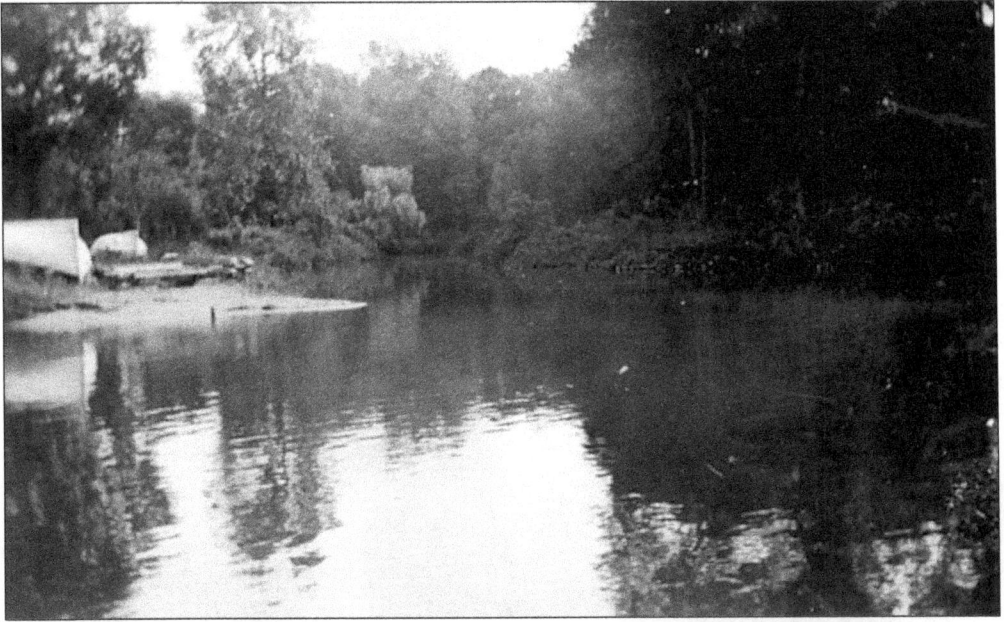

The Lagoons were another early Boeckling innovation. Originally intended for leisurely canoe rides, the lagoons also served as a waterway to haul coal to the Cedar Point power plant.

The original bay pier was enlarged, and pavilions were erected for the comfort of people waiting for ferries. Wooden arches with colored lights led nighttime visitors from the pier to the main resort area near the Grand Pavilion.

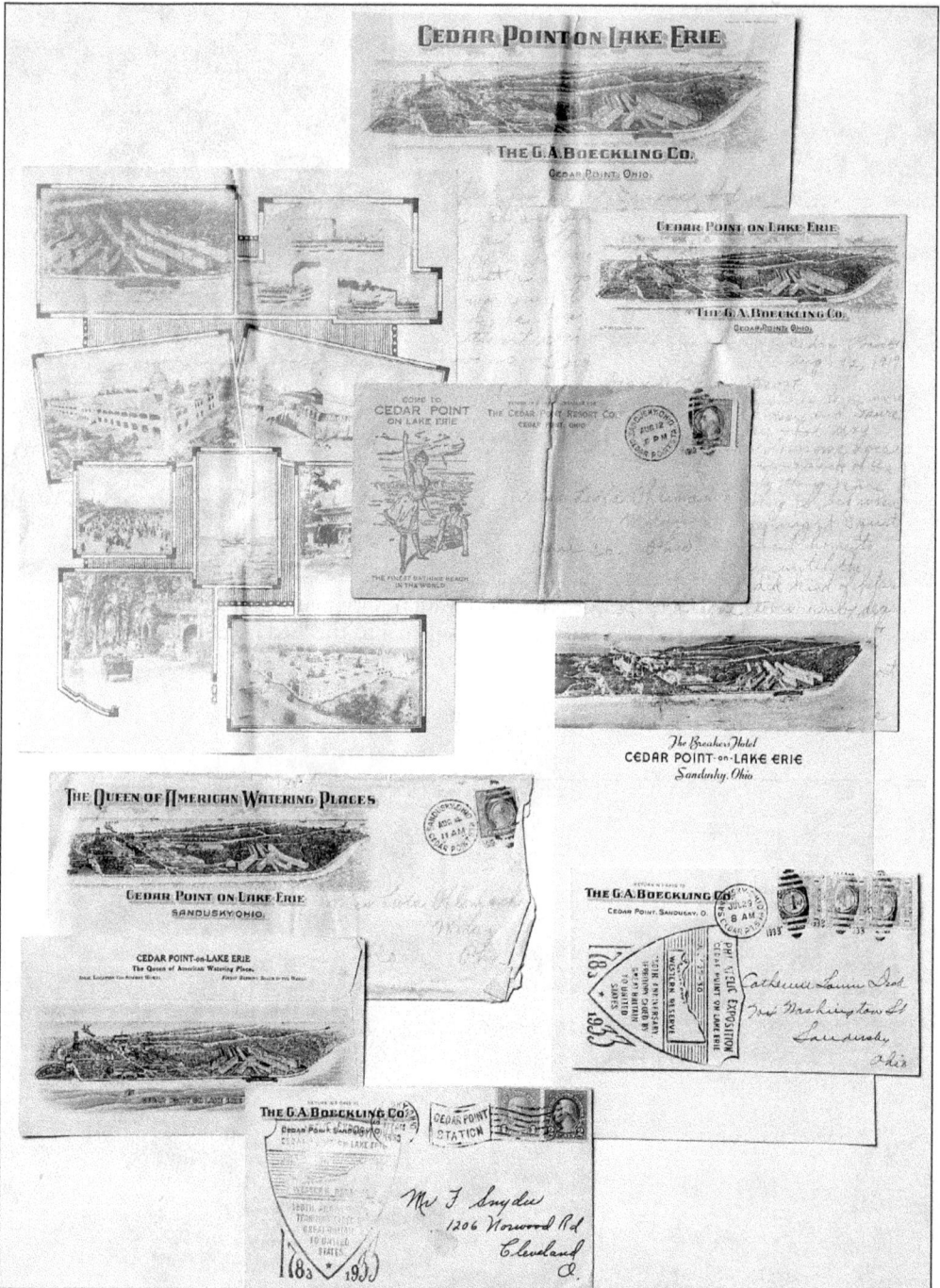

Every letter that left Cedar Point was a miniature advertising billboard. Boeckling was fond of aerial views of the growing resort and featured them on letterheads and envelopes for 30 years.

Two

THE QUEEN OF AMERICAN WATERING PLACES

1905–1918

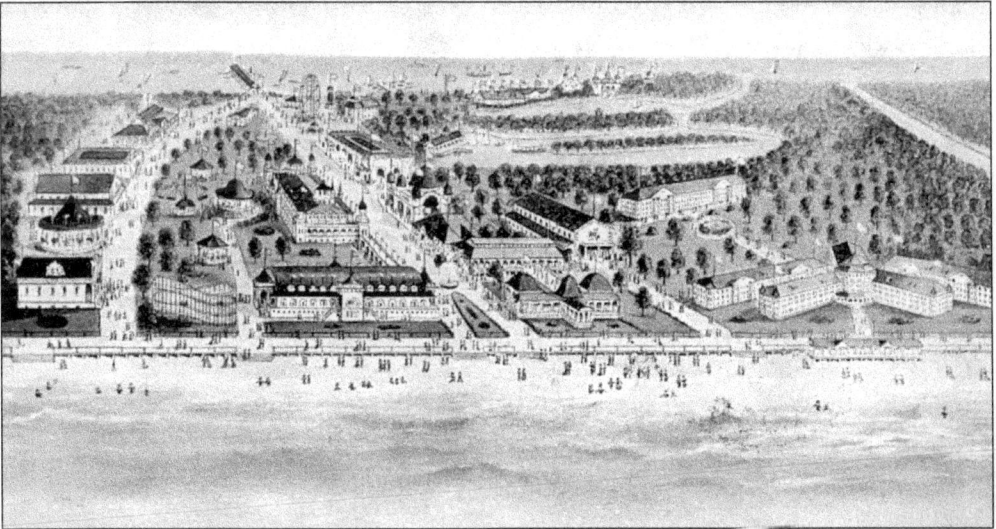

By 1906, Cedar Point was a magical land of elaborate buildings, rambling hotels, cavernous beer gardens, first class restaurants, amusement rides, games, exhibits, souvenir shops, and theatres. Although this artist's conception of the resort was not totally accurate (the Ferris wheel near the bay never existed), it successfully portrays the spirit of Cedar Point under Boeckling's direction.

Opened in June of 1905, the Hotel Breakers was Boeckling's crowning achievement. He spared no expense to make the Breakers one of the great resort hotels. Services included a physician, beautician, manicurist, stenographer, tailor, barber, photographic darkroom, cigar and newsstand, souvenir counter, and ice cream parlor.

A central feature of Hotel Breakers was its lofty rotunda. It was in this rotunda that President William Howard Taft took his dinner in 1913, where John Philip Sousa relaxed with a cigar, where Ernestine Schumann-Heink sang a few impromptu opera selections, and where future Hollywood star Tyrone Power played as a child. (Cedar Point Archives.)

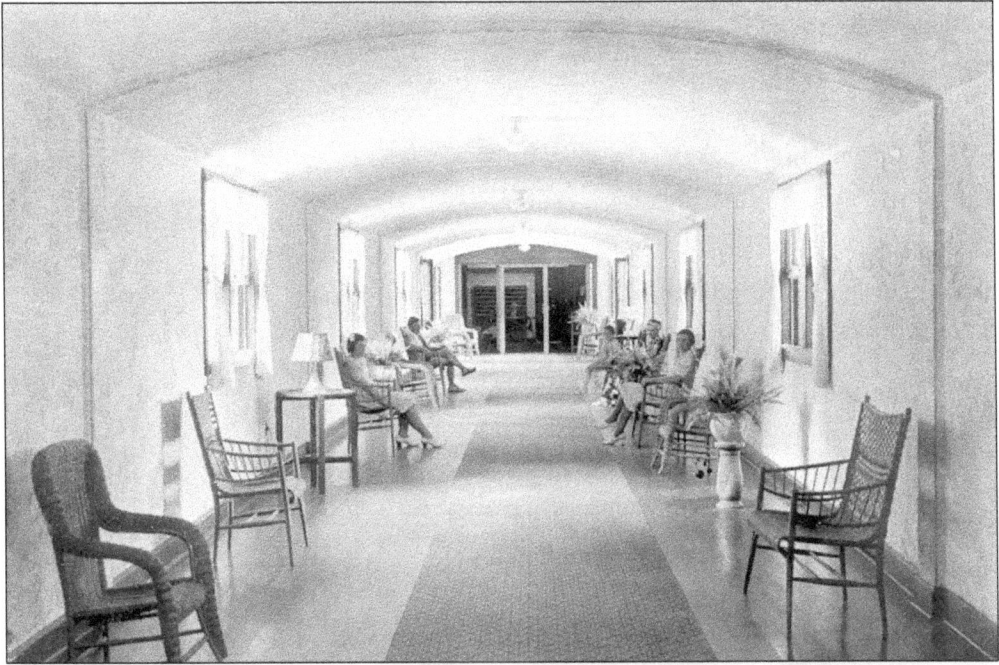

Wide, breezy corridors connected the sections of the hotel with the lobby and the rotunda. Like the sleeping rooms, the public spaces were filled with wicker furniture that Boeckling imported from Austria. (Cedar Point Archives.)

By the resort standards of the early 1900s, the rooms at Hotel Breakers were fairly luxurious. Every room was fitted with running water, and some even had baths. The décor in the hotel rooms remained essentially unchanged for half a century.

Trees shade the entrance to the White House Hotel during the 1910 season. Five years later, the White House became part of the new Cedars Hotel. These buildings survived and now serve as employee dormitories.

The fourth hotel built during the Boeckling era was the Cedars, which opened in 1915. Situated on the bay shore, and incorporating the White House Hotel, the Cedars featured 270 guest rooms, a cafeteria, a gift shop, cigar stand, cozy corners with writing tables, and stained glass windows created by the Louis Comfort Tiffany studio.

32

A narrow gauge freight railroad facilitated easy transport of supplies and luggage from the pier to the hotels and other resort buildings. Unlike the passenger railroads built during the 1960s, this railroad did not carry resort guests.

As the resort expanded, the need for a new Administration Building was constructed to keep pace with the needs of the expanding resort. Before he built his cottage near the lake shore, George Boeckling lived in an apartment on the second floor of the Administration Building. During Prohibition, Federal Agents uncovered a sizeable stock of illegal liquor secreted away in the building for Boeckling's "favored guests." (Cedar Point Archives.)

A bright future for Cedar Point hinged on a reliable source of electricity. To meet the resort's demand, a powerhouse was built in 1906. Located near the lagoons, the building housed coal-fired boilers, a Brush dynamo, and the equipment to control and distribute power throughout the resort and to summer cottages. The power plant generally operated throughout the year.

The Coliseum, which debuted in 1906, was a massive 90,000-square-foot structure that featured a ballroom/concert facility on the top floor and a huge Rathskeller on the main floor. The Rathskeller's manager employed college students to dispense beer, wine, and liquor to thirsty visitors. During a few seasons, waiters wore roller skates to expedite service.

Night Scene on the largest Dance Floor on Lake Erie, Cedar Point, Ohio.

The Coliseum's ballroom claimed to be "The Largest Dancing Pavilion on the Great Lakes." Claims that the dance floor could accommodate 10,000 dancers were exaggerated, but it could comfortably seat 2,000 for concerts like those featuring Leopold Adler's Cedar Point Band. When the so-called indecent "new" dances became popular around 1915, many were banned at the Coliseum's ballroom.

Interior of Souvenir Pavilion and Postal Shop, Cedar Point, O.

By 1913, Cedar Point was attracting 1,000,000 guests per year. It's safe to say that the majority of them wanted souvenirs of their vacations at Cedar Point. George Boeckling happily met the demand for mementoes of his resort by putting gift shops in the hotels. He also added a postcard stand and a large souvenir pavilion that offered a broad and (hopefully) irresistible array of china, glassware, leather goods, postcards, beach supplies, and toys.

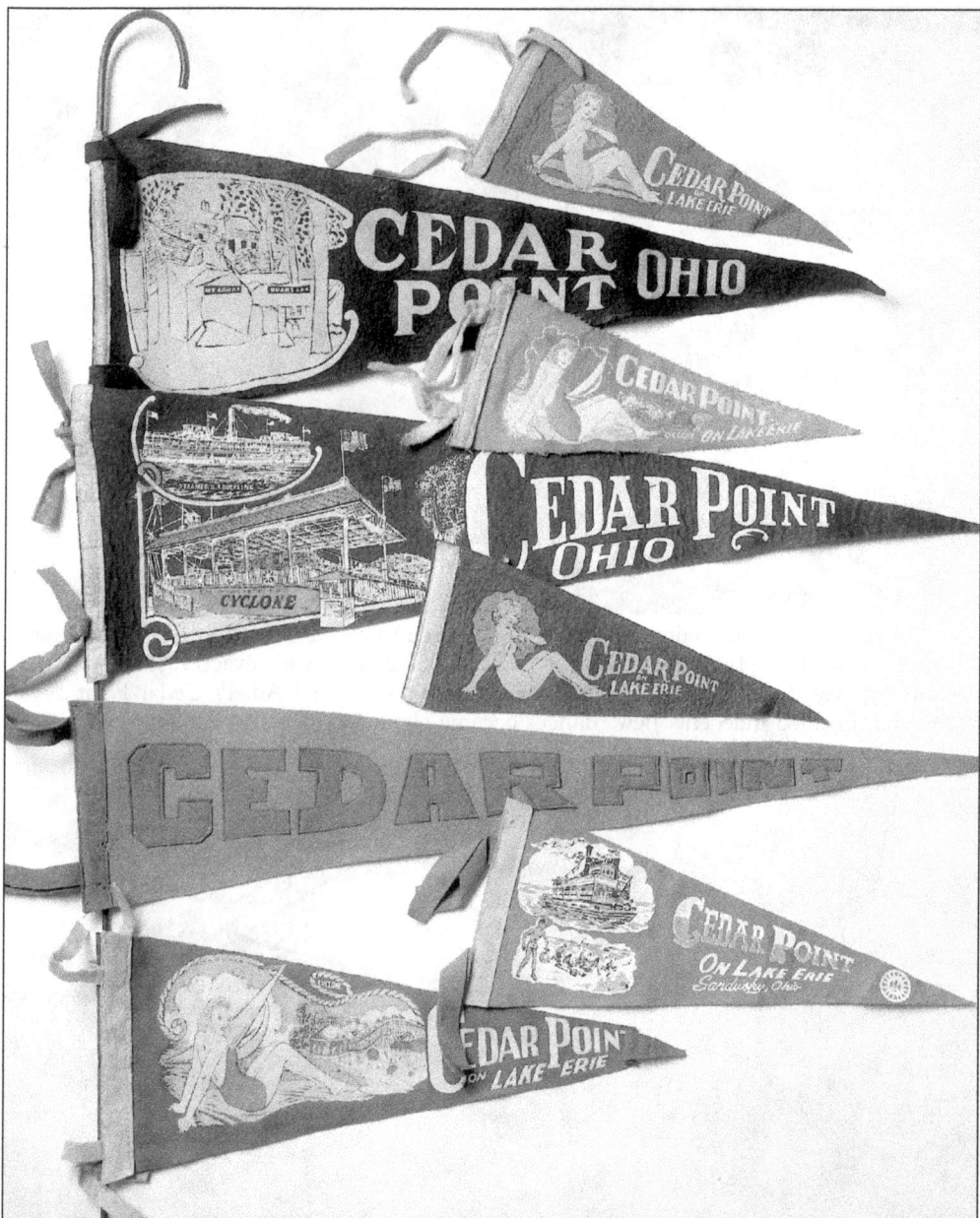

Felt pennants have been favorite souvenirs of Cedar Point for more than 100 years. Available in an endless selection of sizes, colors, and designs, these pennants featured bathing beauties, hotels, rides, or just the words, "Cedar Point." They were sometimes sold with bamboo canes, and the largest pennants measure about three feet in length.

Postcards were first sold at Cedar Point c. 1898. During the decades since, literally millions have been bought and sent. Over the years, postcards of Cedar Point have been offered as single views, in folders and packets, and even in miniature cloth postal bags for safe mailing.

Today, collectors of Cedar Pont memorabilia especially treasure non-souvenir items such as taffy boxes depicting scenes of the resort. During the 1910s, the Cedar Point Candy Co. produced taffy in flavors such as pecan, strawberry, chocolate, and vanilla, but black walnut taffy was always the resort's top-seller.

Although George Boeckling did not admire amusement parks, he recognized their popularity and profitability. Accordingly, he introduced an Amusement Circle in 1906 that stretched from the bay shore to the beach. This early view shows the Japanese Tea Gardens and the Japanese Rolling Ball game.

Near the center of the new Amusement Circle was a bowling alley equipped with modern, automatic pin-setters. Although women were welcome, the bowling alleys primarily attracted male visitors.

The centerpiece of the new Amusement Circle was the Circle Swing, built and operated by the Ingersoll Engineering and Constructing Co. of Pittsburgh. Fred Ingersoll was the builder of the 1902 Figure 8 Roller Toboggan; he was associated with Cedar Point for several decades. Behind the Circle Swings can be seen the Arcade, Chateau Alphonse (a funhouse), and Hale's Tours of the World. (Cedar Point Archives.)

Carousels had been in operation at Cedar Point since the 1880s, but the first large carousel to appear at the resort was installed on the new Amusement Circle in 1906. The new carousel was built and operated by the T.M. Harton Co., who operated rides in many parks and also owned West View Park near Pittsburgh as well as a Cedar Point roller coaster. Harton remained a Cedar Point concessionaire for three decades. (Cedar Point Archives.)

Harton's carousel was a menagerie machine, featuring a wide variety of animals in addition to the traditional horses. Harton hired Daniel Muller, an important Philadelphia carousel carver, to carve all of the animals for the Cedar Point ride. Muller returned to the resort years later to repair and embellish some of the animals.

The Harton Co. constructed the large Leap the Dips roller coaster for the 1912 season. The ride was designed by Erwin Vettel, a prolific coaster engineer of the early 20th century. The Leap the Dips closed around 1935 and was demolished a few years later.

The manager of the Leap the Dips roller coaster and the ride's ticket seller relax briefly on the steps of the coaster's station. In those days, patrons and ride operators alike dressed rather formally. A long-sleeved shirt, celluloid collar, tie, and vest would not have been comfortable at any time let alone a hot and humid day in July!

Joining the Amusement Circle in 1908, the Dip the Dips Scenic Railway was 4,500 feet long. It provided a fairly fast and exciting ride for just 10¢. Located at the center of the Amusement Circle, the ride's attractive station was outlined in colored lights that provided an impressive display for nighttime operations.

After the 1917 season, the Dip the Dips was rebuilt and enlarged. In addition, the station was modified and expanded. At that time, the ride's name was changed to Speed-O-Plane, and a few seasons later, the name was changed again to the Leap Frog Railway. Rebuilt yet again in 1934, it reopened as the High Frolics coaster. It finally closed forever in 1940. (Cedar Point Archives.)

Tickets or season passes could be bought for steamship passage from Sandusky across the bay to Cedar Point. Once at the resort, individual ride and attraction tickets were required, and game winners could redeem tickets and coupons for exciting prizes.

Even though it was only at the resort for one season, this wild animal show featured an elaborately carved entrance. At center stage, a "talker," a clown and a trained-dog act, work to lure customers into the show, while a brassy military band organ plays marches and popular tunes.

During the 1907 season, a troupe of Igorrotes from Luzon made their home in a specially constructed village at Cedar Point. The show was typical of the ethnological exhibits that appeared at World's Fairs, amusement parks, and summer resorts during the early 1900s. After their summer at Cedar Point, the Igorrotes appeared at the Ohio State Fair and then moved on to Chicago's White City Park in 1908. (Cedar Point Archives.)

On August 31, 1910, pioneer aviator Glenn Curtiss set a new over-water flight record by flying from Cleveland's Euclid Beach Park to Cedar Point's beach in one hour and 17 minutes. More than 10,000 people gathered to see the historical landing. Curtiss flew back to Cleveland the following day and returned to Cedar Point in 1911 to give exhibition flights.

AND

Matt Hinkel declared Chaney out at 2 m. 27 s.

JOHNNY KILBANE DEFENDING THE FEATHERWEIGHT CHAMPIONSHIP OF THE WORLD BY KNOCKING OUT GEORGE CHANEY IN THE 3RD ROUND AT CEDAR POINT, LABOR DAY, SEPTEMBER 4TH, 1916

Cedar Point hosted three major boxing matches between 1915 and 1920. On September 4, 1916, Cleveland's Featherweight Champion of the World, Johnny Kilbane, defeated challenger George Chaney. Kilbane scored a knockout in the third round in a 6,000-seat arena near the bay dock. (Cedar Point Archives.)

45

In 1910, the old bathhouse was replaced with a new facility that covered four acres of sand and contained 1,000 tiny rooms where swimmers could change clothes and store possessions. "Key girls" were paid 50¢ a day to lock and unlock the changing rooms while hoping for supplemental tips from appreciative customers.

The new bathhouse was advertised as the largest in the world. Among the amenities offered were towel rentals, swimsuit rentals, and a sales counter where swimmers could purchase suits, bathing shoes, and other items. Rental suits were laundered each night in large washers and dryers.

On a busy day at the beach, a lifeguard stands watch next to his surfboat. Cedar Point's most famous lifeguard was the legendary Notre Dame football coach, Knute Rockne. Rockne worked at Cedar Point in 1913 and returned to the point as a visitor many times before his death in 1931.

The bathing beauties of the 1910s wore more revealing swimsuits than had their mothers, but the heavy woolen garments were still not particularly attractive. If the young lady in the front row really was a lifeguard, Cedar Point would have been one of the first American resorts to employ female beach patrol personnel. Most resorts did not hire female lifeguards until after World War II.

When old Cedar Point was at the height of its popularity, the beach could become so crowded that there was literally "standing room only." The few bathers that were fortunate enough to find a few feet of unoccupied sand could protect themselves from the sun with rented umbrellas.

Not everyone came to Cedar Point to relax or play. The resort required a large staff to operate and maintain the facility to Boeckling's demanding standards. Here, resort carpenter Fred Laepply takes a break while working on a small building.

The neatly attired cafeteria crew poses with their manager during the summer of 1913. The employee in the circle is Bonnie Skiles, who met Knute Rockne that summer at Cedar Point. They were married in Sandusky after Rockne's graduation from Notre Dame in 1914.

In the main dining room of the Grand Pavilion, a small army of hostesses, waitresses, and bus boys await the evening dinner crowd. Although there was no air conditioning, ceiling fans and open windows facing Lake Erie usually kept the restaurant reasonably comfortable.

Recognizing that the automobile would eventually become the main mode of transportation to Cedar Point, Boeckling constructed an auto road in 1914. The new road connected the resort area with the "mainland," and on July 4, 1916, an estimated 2,000 cars traveled the seven miles from the road's entrance to the resort grounds. Parking garages and gasoline stations were also built at Cedar Point.

The Lake Shore Electric Railway, a high-speed interurban line, annually brought thousands of Cedar Point visitors to Sandusky from Toledo, Cleveland, Lorain, Elyria, and other communities. L.S.E. passengers bound for Cedar Point were transported to the foot of Columbus Avenue in Sandusky to make connections with one of the Cedar Point ferries.

Around 1910, a New York Central excursion train waits while passengers de-train and walk to the Cedar Point dock (left). At the right, the steamer *Arrow* prepares for a trip to the Lake Erie islands. On one Sunday in 1908, 16 trains jammed the spurs near the Cedar Point dock as thousands of excursionists made their way to the resort.

In 1907, Boeckling constructed a lake pier, and the steamship *Eastland* initiated daily trips from Cleveland to Cedar Point. During the 1913 season, the *Eastland*'s last year of resort service, she carried 200,000 people to Cedar Point. In 1915, the unstable *Eastland* capsized in the Chicago River, killing more than 800 people.

As the *Eastland* neared the lake pier near the tip of Cedar Point, a steam calliope mounted near the stern of the ship serenaded passengers. The calliope played so loudly that when conditions were right, the music could be heard across the bay in Sandusky.

Using engines from the old steamer *New York*, a new double-ended passenger ferry was built and put into service in 1909. To the surprise of no one, the new steamer was christened the *G.A. Boeckling*. Business at Cedar Point was so good that both the *R.B. Hayes* and the *A. Wehrle Jr.* operated beside the new steamer in order to handle the big crowds.

In this *c.* 1915 photo, the G.A. *Boeckling* lists toward the Sandusky pier as passengers board her for the trip to the resort. At the end of the pier is the resort's utility launch, *Dispatch*. This little vessel was used to transport supplies and employees but was also pressed into passenger service on extremely busy days.

Despite her age, the *R.B. Hayes* was kept in service until almost 1920. On March 25, 1917, she was "on the ways" having all of her hull planking replaced to extend her life. As the automobile rapidly gained popularity, the demand for ferries declined and the G.A. *Boeckling* could handle the dwindling number of steamship passengers by herself.

In 1908, 10-year-old Aileen Foley visited the Cedar Point Photo Co. and posed in her spotless white summer dress on a faux airplane. Other props at the photo studio included a steamship, a railroad passenger car, an automobile, a canoe, and a donkey.

Three

THE LAST YEARS
OF THE GOLDEN AGE
1919–1931

In 1929, the Cedar Point Peninsula still had an abundant growth of shade trees and an unpaved parking lot. The roller coasters are (left to right): the Leap the Dips, the Leap Frog Railway, and the new Cyclone. A large complex of parking garages can be seen near the bay dock and smoke drifts from the stack of the powerhouse (top center).

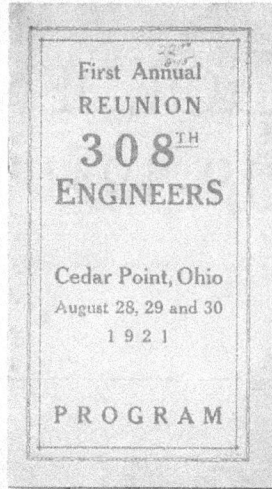

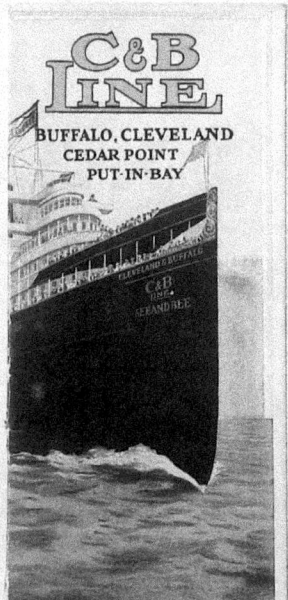

Prohibition took effect at Cedar Point on July 1, 1919. To counter the loss of revenue from beer, wine, and liquor sales, Boeckling sought to attract more visitors through an aggressive advertising campaign. A significant portion of the advertising budget was earmarked for brochures that were mailed to prospective visitors and distributed at events and shows throughout the winter months.

The Cafeteria Moderne in the Grand Pavilion offered visitors faster service and lower prices than the adjacent dining room. Table settings were less formal and the décor was plain compared to the Grill Room, but the cafeteria was popular with families and those with limited budgets.

Meals were prepared in the central kitchen complex for the Grill Room, the Cafeteria Moderne, the employees' cafeteria, and catered events. The resort maintained a large kitchen staff headed by an executive chef. In 1919, one kitchen employee recalled working endless hours in the hot kitchen with only an occasional knife fight between temperamental employees to break the tedium.

After a number of storms, including a damaging one in 1917 that washed out parts of the auto road, Boeckling eliminated the vulnerable section and constructed a new entrance further west. When the new road opened in 1920, a huge illuminated sign welcomed visitors, while a smaller sign advertised the sale of cottage lots along "The Chausee."

By 1915, automobiles were bringing 3,000 people a day to the resort. During the 1920s, this number increased drastically and created a demand for more parking lots and parking garages. Undeveloped areas near the Amusement Circle and picnic grove were converted to parking lots.

On a sunny day in 1927, sand sculptors create works of temporary art on the beach. Note the sun deck that extended over the beach and the stack of beach chairs ready for rental. In the distance is the beach refreshment stand near Hotel Breakers.

The Sea Swing on the beach was a big hit during the 1920s. Powered by a gasoline engine, the ride provided welcome breezes on hot summer days. Heavy woolen swimsuits of the day could fill with water as the ride dragged passengers through the waves. This occurrence occasionally resulted in the embarrassing loss of a suit.

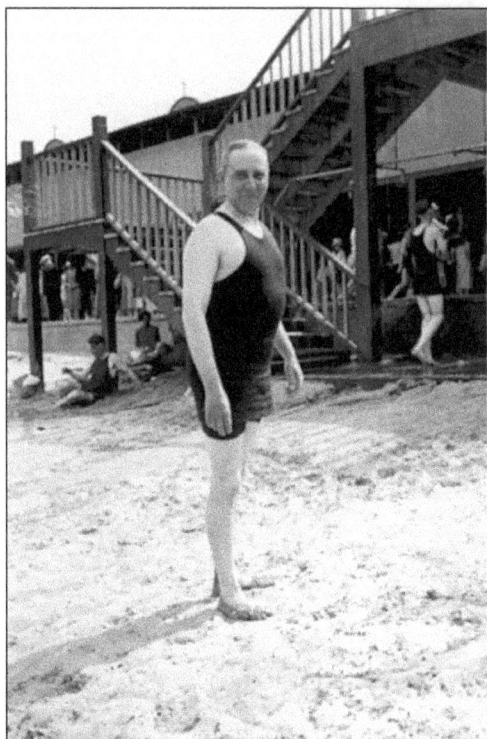

A prominent Akron judge posed in front of the bathhouse during the Akron-Summit County picnic of 1925. Most summer resorts did not permit men to appear on the beach topless until around the time of World War II.

Originally, water toboggans were popular during the 1890s, but they enjoyed a resurgence in the 1920s. Accordingly, Cedar Point installed two new water toboggans next to the sea swing. Because of damage from ice during the winter, water toboggans did not usually survive for many seasons.

The Cleveland & Buffalo Transit Co. placed the steamer *Goodtime* (ex-*City of Detroit II*) on the Cleveland to Cedar Point route in 1925.

Captain Ralph Spurrier was master of the beloved *Goodtime* during her years on the Cedar Point Route. When the C & B Line abandoned passenger service after the 1938 season, the *Goodtime* was offered for sale, but she was too old and worn to interest any buyers and was scrapped a few years later.

All Set For A Meeting, Cedar Point On Lake Erie

The convention hall in the Grand Pavilion was kept busy throughout the 1920s. In 1925, the Lions Club held their national convention at Cedar Point, and Helen Keller challenged 7,500 Lions to establish a program to help prevent blindness and to assist in eye care. The Lions responded with a global commitment to vision health.

The best rooms in the Cedars Hotel faced the bay and cost just $2 a day per person or $12.25 per week. By comparison, a lakefront room in the Breakers was $3.50 a day, and a first-floor parlor room was $10 a day. All rooms were "furnished in attractive and comfortable style," although the Cedars offered no private baths.

Three fashionably dressed young ladies pose on the "Lover's Bridge" in 1921. Located not far from the Coliseum, this wooden bridge was especially popular with the so-called "summer girls," who came to Cedar Point each season in search of a husband.

Gasoline engine lagoon barges carried visitors from the lake dock near the tip of the peninsula to the center of the resort near the Crystal Rock Castle and the powerhouse.

Workers at Cedar Point were required to abide by rules published in a manual "governing the Deportment of Employees." When off duty, however, they were encouraged to take advantage of the resort as if they were visitors. In this photo, a group of well-dressed employees pose near one of the many metal statues that Boeckling purchased in 1905.

With Lake Erie in the background, resort visitors stroll along the Amusement Circle in search of thrills and entertainment. This photo was taken from the roof of the Leap Frog Railway. In the little ticket booth, an employee sells admission to the Tumble Inn, one of Cedar Point's funhouses.

To the left of the Leap Frog Railway station is the building that housed the Cascades, a flume-type water ride with boats that cruised slowly along narrow channels. The Cedar Point Candy Co. sold black walnut taffy in one of the front corners of the Cascades building; beyond the Cascades was the Tumble Inn funhouse.

Noah's Ark, a unique rocking funhouse, was installed on the Cedar Point midway in 1925. Leroy Raymond of Ocean Beach, California, designed the first Noah's Ark in 1917. In partnership with carousel builder William H. Dentzel, Raymond formed the Noah's Ark Corporation and sold Arks to parks throughout the world. In 2004, only two Noah's Arks still survive. (Toledo-Lucas County Public Library.)

The Concourse building was constructed to house a series of games, including some games of chance that rarely awarded prizes. In front of the Concourse are the flower gardens that were a hallmark of Cedar Point during the Boeckling era.

Some of Cedar Point's concessionaires remained at the resort for decades. Others stayed just one season, and each spring Boeckling advertised in *Billboard* magazine to attract new concessions. These "Old Fashioned" silhouette artists set up business on a portable table under an umbrella and paid Boeckling a flat fee for the privilege of operating along the midway.

In 1929, as in 2004, roller coasters towered above the resort, and the joyful screams of riders echoed through the midway. The Leap the Dips is in the foreground, the Leap Frog Railway in the center, and the new Cyclone is seen along the lakeshore. (Cedar Point Archives.)

The legendary Cyclone roller coaster (left) was built in 1929 for the Cedar Point Coaster Co., one of a number of companies founded by Boeckling and operated essentially as subsidiaries of the G.A. Boeckling Co. Others were the Cedar Point Hotel Co., the Bay Transportation Co., the Cedar Point Bridge Co., and the Lake Erie Building Co. (Cedar Point Archives.)

The Cyclone was designed by Fred Church, one of the most innovative and daring of all roller coaster engineers. It was built by Harry Traver, a well-known amusement ride designer and builder. Traver also developed the Circle Swing and the Tumble Bug rides. (Cedar Point Archives.)

"Scientifically Built for Speed," the Cyclone provided sheer terror for riders. Twisting, turning, and bone-jarring, Church's violent ride featured steep drops, sharply-banked turns, and spiraling descents. Many riders tried the Cyclone once and never returned. The Cyclone would be George Boeckling's last major contribution to Cedar Point.

On February 2, 1929, his 67th birthday, George Boeckling posed at his Columbus Avenue home with his sister Elizabeth and his pet dog, Laddie. Seriously ill, he was bedridden on the opening day of the 1929 season. Confined to a wheelchair, he paid his final visit to Cedar Point on July 4, 1931. He died on July 24, 1931, just as the Great Depression deepened, and the resort most needed his leadership.

Four

DEPRESSION, WAR, AND A RESORT IN DECLINE
1932–1945

Following the death of George Boeckling in 1931, Edward A. Smith became Cedar Point's general manager and was later elected president of the G.A. Boeckling Co. In 1905, Smith had abandoned his career as a banker and joined Boeckling's organization as Boeckling's "right hand man." Smith directed Cedar Point through nearly 20 difficult years of depression and war. He finally retired in 1949—a time when Cedar Point's future was very tenuous.

Despite the best efforts of Ed Smith, the G.A. Boeckling Co. did not report a profit for the seasons from 1932 to 1949. As a result, maintenance on both buildings and rides was minimal for several years. In this photo, taken near the Beachcomber refreshment stand, the famous wooden boardwalk is clearly in desperate need of repair.

In 1932, Frederick Posner leased the aging Crystal Rock Castle and converted it into a sandwich shop that specialized in hot corned beef sandwiches. After the repeal of Prohibition, beer, ale, wine, and liquors joined Coca-Cola on the menu.

When Prohibition ended, Ed Smith established the Terrace Tavern near Hotel Breakers. Offering live music in the evening, the outdoor tavern served a wide range of beverages that included the Breakers Cocktail, Cedar Point Special pilsner beer, and bottles of Cedar Point ginger ale. (Cedar Point Archives.)

In Hotel Breakers, the Lobby Grill served breakfast, lunch, and late evening sandwiches. Many patrons visited the Lobby Grill for a cold bottle of beer on a hot summer day. In many ways, the return of alcohol sales probably helped keep Cedar Point alive during the worst years of the 1930s. An illegal gambling operation in the hotel also may have helped.

The Great Depression was a disaster for amusement parks and summer resorts. Scores of great summer hotels closed and were demolished during the decade, but the Hotel Breakers managed to keep its doors open. The condition of the hotel declined, however, and holes appeared in screens, paint flaked, and ancient mattresses provided guests with numerous back aches. (Cedar Point Archives.)

Much of the furniture at Hotel Breakers during the 1930s and 1940s was the same furniture bought for the grand opening in June of 1905. Ed Smith provided a clean hotel, but worn furniture, rugs, and bed linens underlined the fact that both the Breakers and Cedar Point were in deep financial trouble.

While Hotel Breakers still welcomed guests, the Cedars Hotel was closed to the public when business declined. A few guests were sent to the Cedars on rare occasions when the Breakers was full, but the Cedars was largely used as an employee dormitory and quarters for the annual Ohio Band Camp.

With business declining due to the Depression, the pace of life at Cedar Point in the 1930s was markedly slower than it had been in the 1920s. Leisurely tennis matches on the courts near Hotel Breakers were a popular afternoon pastime, as was horseback riding or a canoe ride on the lagoons.

During the 1920s, as many as 1,000 automobiles a day created traffic jams along the Chausee. In the mid-1930s, however, the entrance road stood empty and sand-covered. Those who did manage to visit Cedar Point were greeted by the sight of the majestic Cyclone coaster as they entered the resort grounds. (Cedar Point Archives.)

On the midway, the once glistening Eden Musee showed signs of rust dripping down the metal façade when owners could not afford a coat of paint. This excellent wax museum originally operated in Boston and was moved to Cedar Point in 1918. It displayed wax figures of famous people, notorious criminals, and the obligatory Chamber of Horrors. (Toledo-Lucas County Public Library.)

THE BUG-1942

The tumble Bug ride, installed in 1934, was one of the few midway additions to Cedar Point during the '30s. Designed and built by the Traver Engineering Co. of Beaver Falls, Pennsylvania, the Tumble Bug was a mainstay of amusement park midways from the 1920s to the 1960s.

Situated in a distinctive circular structure, the Penny Arcade and Skee Ball alleys were operated by John Berni and his wife. Skee Ball players received nine balls for 5¢. At this time, many arcade machines still cost just a penny to play.

A ride on the Leap the Dips coaster was only 15¢ during the early 1930s. Even so, few people could afford to spend much on amusement rides. The T.M. Harton Co. found it difficult to operate and maintain both the Leap the Dips and their carousel. In 1922, the carousel grossed a respectable $3,500, but by 1933, ticket sales did not even cover the expenses of operation.

The once magnificent Leap the Dips coaster was abandoned by its owners in 1935 and stood idle until demolished a few years later. The seat cushions from the trains and various other items were salvaged and used on the new High Frolics coaster. The High Frolics was a rebuilt version of the Leap Frog Railway that opened in 1934.

With both the *R.B. Hayes* and the *A. Wehrle Jr.* retired and dismantled, the *G.A. Boeckling* was the only remaining vessel of the Bay Transportation Co. In this 1930s view, the captain supervises docking and the lowering of the gangplanks as a small crowd waits to board for a morning trip to the Sandusky dock.

On quiet days, it was not difficult to obtain permission from the captain to take a photo in front of one of the wheelhouses of the *G.A. Boeckling*. Unlike the resort, the *Boeckling* was well maintained to pass the annual inspections required by the Steamboat Inspection Service and later, the United States Coast Guard. If the ship failed an inspection, she could not operate.

The exterior of the Cafeteria and the main dining room were essentially unchanged and still exhibited Boeckling's touch in the graceful statuary on the roof. Inside, the old Grill Room, now known as the Green and Silver Grill, was renovated and redecorated in art deco style. The restaurant continued its tradition of high culinary standards under the direction of Chef Henri Rigo. (Cedar Point Archives.)

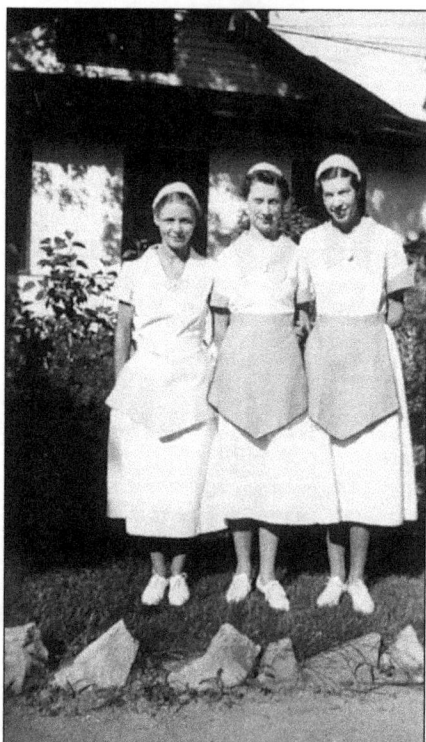

Cedar Point has always provided summer employment for college students. In 1936, these three waitresses from Ohio University helped pay their college expenses by working in the Green and Silver Grill. The restaurant was closed from 2:30 p.m. to 5:30 p.m., allowing time for tennis, swimming, or enjoying midway attractions with other employees.

GREEN AND SILVER GRILL
Cedar Point on Lake Erie
=== **DINNER** ===

LUNCHEON   Monday, June 29, 1936   **DINNER**

11:00 A.M. TO 2:30 P.M.   5:30 TO 9:00 P.M.

CHEF RIGO'S FAMOUS FOODS KNOWN FROM COAST TO COAST

Fresh Caught Fish and Fresh Lobsters Arrive Daily

CHOICE OF SOUP or APPETIZER: Fruit Cocktail   Chilled Tomato Juice
   Chicken Mulligatawny   Cottage Cheese   Pineapple Juice
   Mamas Chicken and Beef Pot au Feu Soup   Bismark Herring   Roll Mops
   Clam Chowder, Manhattan   Chicken, Beef or Tomato Essense in Jelly
   Chicken Noodle Soup   Chopped Liver   Sauerkraut Juice
      Radishes, Green Onions, Pickles, Cucumber Slices

FISH ENTREES or ROASTS:
French Fried Whole Sole, Butter, Colbert 1.00   *Sea Mussel, Mari nere 75
*Broiled Mackerel, Parsley Butter Sauce 75   *Fried Perch, Sauce Remoulade 75
*Fried Whole Weakfish Sauce Remoulade 75   Fried Scallops, Sauce Remulade 95
Fried Soft Shell Crabs, Sauce Tartar(2) 95   *Steamed Chicken Lobster, Melted Butter 1.35
Broiled Baby Lobster Melted Butter 1.50   Real Main Lobster Newburg 1.75
Lake Whitefish, Sweet Sour Raisin Sauce 95   One Dozen Frog Legs Fried, Sauce Tartar 1.50
French Jumbo Frog in Butter, Grenoibloise 1.50   *Chicken Chow Mein, Fried Noodles 95
Shirred Eggs with Sausage, Bercy 75   *German Beef Sauerbraten, Potato Pancake 85
   *Combination Lamb, Veal, Beef and Pork Hochpot Stew, Boiled Dumplings 75
   *Boiled Fresh Prime Beef Brisket, Horsaradish Sauce, Vegetable Cabbage 75
   *Individual Prime Short Rib Fresh Vegetables, Cocotte 85
   *Roast Loin of Pork, Caraway Gravy, Lyonnaise Mashed Potatoe 85
Broiled Tenderloin Steak Chow Chow Sauce 1.00
*Roast English Leg of Lamb Mint Sauce 1.00   Broiled Lamb Chops, French Fried Onions 95
*Roast Celery fed Duckling, Goose Liver Dressing, Compote 1.00
*Roast Stuffed Chicken (half) Dressing, Giblet Sauce 1.25
*Roast Vermont Turkey, Goose Liver Dressing, Giblet Sauce, Cranberry Jelly 1.50
*Roast Prime Rib of Beef, Yorkshire Pudding, Gravy 1.25
Prime Beef Tenderloin, Fresh Mushrooms 1.50   Prime Sirloin Steak, Maitre d'Hotel 1.10
Porterhouse Steak Charcoal Broiled, Parsley Butter Sauce 2.00
      Choice of Delicious Salads

POTATOES and VEGETABLES: New Bermuda Potatoes in Cream,   Shoestring
French Fried,   Hashed Brown Potatoes,   Mashed,   Plain Boiled,   Hashed in Cream
New String Beans   New Carrots   Cauliflower   New Peas   Fried Sweet Potatoes
   Buttered New Turnips   New Beets   Spinach   Early York Cabbage

D E S S E R T S:
   Orange or Pineapple Sherbet   Watermelon   Melon a la Mode   Raspberry Parfait
   Chocolate, Vanilla, Strawberry Ice Cream   Mixed Jello, Whipped Cream
Fresh Apple   Pineapple   Grapenut Custard Pies   Sliced Peaches, Cream
   Deep Dish Fresh Peach Pie   Bread and Butter Pudding Marischino Sauce
      Chocolate Pecan Cake

BEVERAGES: Glass of, Iced Tea or Coffee   Welsh Grape Punch   Milk or Buttermilk
  Breads and Rolls: Rye   Pumpernikel   Parker House   Soda Biscuits
      Corn Bread   Hard Rolls   Wholewheat Rolls

On Monday, June 29, 1936, Chef Rigo offered an impressive selection of entrees. A broiled lobster was priced at $1.50, while charcoal broiled Porterhouse steaks cost $2. Hod Wiley's Orchestra supplied the music for dinner dancing throughout the evening hours.

While on duty, Cedar Point employees were required to present a neat, clean appearance. Waitresses wore white dresses, aprons, and caps, while hostesses wore conservative dresses. The resort operated a large steam laundry, and employees obtained clean uniforms from a laundry office near the dormitories.

Off duty, employees could sunbathe, swim, play football on the beach, or enjoy a summer romance. However, employees were required to be in their dormitories by 1:00 a.m., and smoking, alcohol, gambling, and profanity were strictly forbidden in the rooms. Employees were paid twice a month, ate in an employees' cafeteria, and had access to a nurse or doctor at all times. Most employees considered Cedar Point a great place to work.

The Ohio Band Camp was an important event at Cedar Point every August from 1932 to 1944. The band provided music for a daily flag raising and offered free concerts at the resort. In 1939, Irene Kvetko of Baldwin-Wallace College led the drum major training class. (Irene Leeds Collection.)

The advent of the Big Band Era helped to keep Cedar Point's gates open during the late 1930s and early '40s. For the 1939 season, Ed Smith renovated the ballroom and had it decorated in art deco style. Over the next decade, the old Coliseum echoed the music of the nation's top bands, including Benny Goodman, Glen Gray, Orin Tucker, the Dorseys, Ted Weems, Tony Pastor, Henry Busse, Ben Bernie, Gene Krupa, and Bob Chester. (Cedar Point Archives.)

On a warm summer morning in 1941, passengers hurry down Cleveland's East 9th Street Pier to catch the sailing of the *Eastern States* bound for Cedar Point. The Detroit & Cleveland Navigation Co. took over the Cleveland-Cedar Point route in 1939 after the demise of the *Goodtime*. Poor patronage forced the D & C Line to abandon the service after the 1942 season. For the first time since 1907, there would be no steamship service from Cleveland to Cedar Point.

In the spring of 1942, the G.A. *Boeckling* awaits the June 13th opening of the season. To the left of the Sandusky pier are the winter offices of the G.A. Boeckling Co. Both the office building and the pier were constructed after the infamous 1924 tornado destroyed the original Sandusky docks.

World War II restrictions created many difficulties for amusement parks and summer resorts. A major hardship was the shortage of manpower. In 1943, Al Berardi, whose parents owned the famous French fry stand at Cedar Point, stood on the deck of the *Boeckling* as he left for military service.

The secluded Cedar Point lagoons were especially popular with servicemen and their dates. On the right is the coal dock and large piles of coal destined for the boiler at the powerhouse.

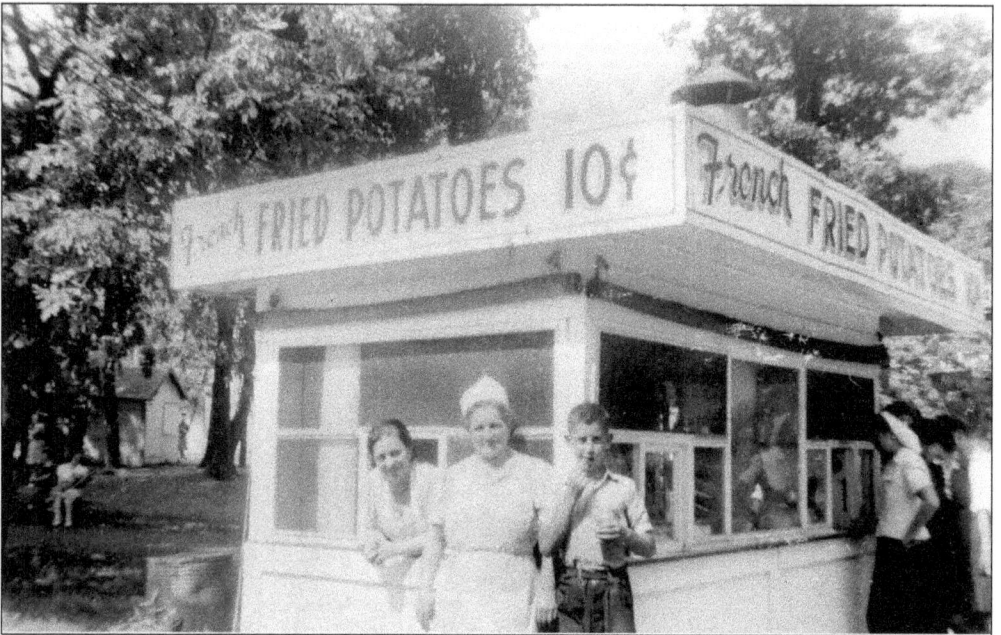

Albert Berardi and Howard Berni, both sons of concessionaires, opened a French fry stand in 1942. A year later, "Momma" Berardi took over the stand, and her French fries became the most famous food at Cedar Point. For more than two decades, few people visited the resort without sampling some of Momma's great fries.

While Momma Berardi sliced and fried potatoes, Secondo Berardi worked behind the stand washing enough potatoes to keep up with demand. Secondo worked for the G.A. Boeckling Co. and also became a ride owner and operator during the 1940s.

The Coffelt Candy Co. replaced the old Cedar Point Candy Co. Besides selling salt water taffy Coffelt's also operated a popcorn stand. Like its predecessor, Coffelt's offered a half dozen flavors of taffy, but found that black walnut was always the top seller. Next to the Coffelt stand was the Kentucky Derby racing game.

During the early 1900s, taffy was pulled by hand, but by the 1940s, the machine between these two Coffelt Candy Co. employees automatically pulled the taffy until it was ready to be placed in a machine that cut and wrapped each piece individually. The taffy was then displayed behind glass and sold in one-pound boxes. Customers could buy one flavor or an assortment of their choice.

Kiddie rides began appearing at Cedar Point during the 1920s. By 1944, the resort operated a Kiddieland that offered a number of rides including a miniature Ferris wheel. To the right of the Ferris wheel is the station for the miniature steam train.

By the late 1930s, the economy was improving and concessionaires installed new rides. An early version of the Moon Rocket, a ride that became very popular during the 1950s, was in operation near the end of the war years.

The Flying Skooter ride was invented by Alvin Bisch in 1934 and was one of the first aerial devices that gave riders a degree of control. The Flying Skooter was brought to Cedar Point by Joseph and Florence Santi, who also owned a food concession on the midway.

The Eyerly Aircraft Co. introduced the Octopus to the park industry in 1934, and Secondo Berardi installed one of these popular rides next to the carousel building in 1941. A year later, Berardi also purchased a Tilt-A-Whirl for the midway.

During the 1930s, the midway near the Cyclone roller coaster was expanded with the addition of a small carousel, a Ferris wheel, and a coffee and donut stand. The charming little carousel was built by C.W. Parker of Leavenworth, Kansas. (Cedar Point Archives.)

No matter how much the midway or the hotels changed, the beach remained mostly unchanged. The water toboggans disappeared, but the sea swing and the 1910 bathhouse survived throughout the 1930s and the war years. Umbrella rentals, at 50¢ a day, were still a bargain, and use of the beach was free to all visitors.

Five

THE LONG ROAD
TO RECOVERY
1946–1958

In 1950, Cedar Point was on the verge of extinction. The resort had been leased by hotel magnate T.C. Melrose, who had no interest in the amusement area. Concessionaries like Berardi, Santi, and Al Tedaldi kept the midway going, but the neglected Cyclone roller coaster operated for the last time that season. In 1951, Cedar Point was without a roller coaster for the first time since 1892.

Cedar Point's management continued issuing brochures during the 1940s and 1950s, but economic factors dictated that advertising materials be produced as inexpensively as possible. As a result, they lacked the color and intricate designs of previous years.

After 40 years at Cedar Point, the T.M. Harton Co. removed their carousel, leaving a vacant building. Ed Smith convinced Carl and Richard Holzapfel to purchase and install a new carousel for the 1946 season. The "new" carousel and its Model 153 Wurlitzer Band Organ were placed in the vacated Harton building.

Holzapfel's carousel was built in 1912 by Philadelphia carver Daniel C. Muller and originally installed at Revere Beach, Massachusetts. Eventually, the outer row of horses was removed and the ride was moved to another New England location before being purchased by the Holzapfels.

The Stinson family operated games on the Cedar Point midway for many years. In 1948, the Spill the Milk game offered chalkware dolls and figurines to anyone who could knock over six milk bottles using three baseballs.

By the end of the Second World War, the towers of the old Cascades building had been truncated in order to avoid maintenance costs. The Hi-De-Ho-in-the-Dark operated in the building that had once housed the Cascades water ride.

In 1947, a heavy snowstorm collapsed the roof of the old Eden Musee and damaged many wax figures. The museum was sold to funhouse and dark ride builder Ed Schmid, who refurbished the Eden Musee and expanded it with figures from Coney Island's Eden Musee.

The ravaged Cedar Point midway of 1948 shows the impact of years of poor profits. The aging and worn buildings include Coffelt's taffy stand, a refreshment stand, the funhouse, and the Laff-in-the-Dark, an updated version of the Hi-De-Ho-in-the-Dark. (Larry Wasserman Collection.)

95

During the late 1940s, the resort was so neglected that one concessionaire joked the buildings were held together by nothing more than layers of old paint. With no financing available, the G.A. Boeckling Co. struggled to keep Cedar Point open and by 1949, concluded that the crumbling resort would soon be closed. (Larry Wasserman Collection.)

The Caterpillar was a very popular ride designed by Hyla F. Maynes and installed in many parks before and after the war. In operation, a green canvas top was pulled over the cars, plunging the riders into disorienting darkness while traveling at high speeds. (Larry Wasserman Collection.)

The Kiddieland of the late 1940s had changed little in two decades. Most of the rides were old, worn, and covered with many coats of paint. The concessionaires had little money and no incentive to make improvements. (Larry Wasserman Collection.)

In this 1948 photo, employees stand in front of the cafeteria that they jokingly called "The Gangrene Room." On the right is the Administration Building and in the center are the bicycles used by Ed Smith and other managers to get around the large resort grounds.

Soon after Dan Schneider took over the Cedar Point lease in 1951, improvements began. Although he had few financial resources, Schneider managed to paint, repair, and expand the resort. In this photo, maintenance employees work in front of the battered façade of the Coliseum.

Although many of the games were still the old standards, Schneider painted the old Concourse building bright orange. Schneider reasoned that the garish paint would announce the fact that Cedar Point was being refurbished.

Schneider appointed veteran hotel manager Sam Gerstner to oversee Hotel Breakers and the restaurants. Although the hotel's exterior needed a major renovation, Gerstner concentrated on improving the guest rooms and the public spaces. The new Veranda cocktail lounge and sun deck was equipped with tables, umbrellas, and lounges, while torches provided light and atmosphere in the evenings.

Ed Starr was placed in charge of the amusement section and immediately implemented changes. Old buildings were modernized and painted, while new attractions, rides, and games were installed. Among the new games was an air-conditioned Fascination facility that seated 40 players.

Due to rising costs and the new Federal "Full Crew" regulations, it became necessary to retire and sell the venerable G.A. *Boeckling* after the 1951 season. Three new 65-foot steel ferries were ordered to replace the old steamship. The first of these, the G.A. *Boeckling II*, was christened on June 7, 1952.

After steaming a total of more than 300,000 miles on Sandusky Bay and carrying an uncalculated number of resort passengers, the G.A. *Boeckling* was towed away on July 10, 1952, and became a floating warehouse. Years later, she was returned to Sandusky and was in the process of restoration when a fire destroyed her at a Toledo dock.

100

Although Dan Schneider operated the resort, the G.A. Boeckling Co. maintained full control of the property and the ferry service. The company's board of directors posed on the new ferry *G.A. Boeckling II* in 1952. They were (left to right): Richard Kruse, J. Richard Dorn, Bernie Zeiher (president), and William A. Hiles.

Irving Ross ran a popular lunch stand that specialized in hot corned beef sandwiches and foot long hot dogs. Ross continued to expand his food services during the 1950s and 1960s, eventually building a new "Ross' Lunch" stand.

Ed Starr convinced Leonard Jefferson to open a 10-ride Kiddieland that included a carousel, miniature steam train, kiddie roller coaster, Hodges hand cars, and a number of car, boat, and airplane rides. Unlike the older Kiddieland, Jefferson's replaced bare earth with gravel.

Zouary's old Tumble Inn funhouse, a midway landmark for decades, was remodeled and improved. It reopened as The Krazy Kastle. The funhouse contained a selection of traditional devices like moving floors, tilting stairways, slides, air jet blowholes, and a human roulette wheel. (Larry Wasserman Collection.)

For many years Cedar Point's crowds supported two funhouses. In addition to Tumble Inn, Hilarity Hall was located next to Noah's Ark. During the 1950s, the old Hilarity Hall operated as the Goofy House. (Larry Wasserman Collection.)

Improving business conditions brought two more funhouses to Cedar Point, giving the resort a lineup of four walk-through operations. The Fun House is best remembered for the hideous characters that greeted patrons from the façade. (Larry Wasserman Collection.)

The Fun Parade welcomed ticket purchasers with a sign that read, "Have Fun by the Ton." This funhouse was visible from almost anywhere on the midway because of its vivid color scheme of red, yellow, and blue. (Larry Wasserman Collection.)

Ripley's Believe it or Not! Odditorium appeared on the midway during the 1950s, but did not last many seasons. Like the Bouquet of Life, which displayed fetal development, the Odditorium was probably a little too educational for Cedar Point's thrill-seeking crowds. (Larry Wasserman Collection.)

Animal exhibits had been part of Cedar Point since the early 1900s. Khan-Amaki's jungle show presented large reptiles from Zamboanga, including boa constrictors and a huge lizard named Bogo. Like many side show-type entertainments, the brightly painted façade was more exciting than the exhibits behind the show front. (Larry Wasserman Collection.)

As business improved, Ed Schmid added new figures to the Eden Musee wax museum. In addition, he placed a Conestoga wagon and General Custer's stuffed horse on display to promote the Musee. The entrance to Noah's Ark is to the left of the flagpole and the Ark itself looms in the background. (Larry Wasserman Collection.)

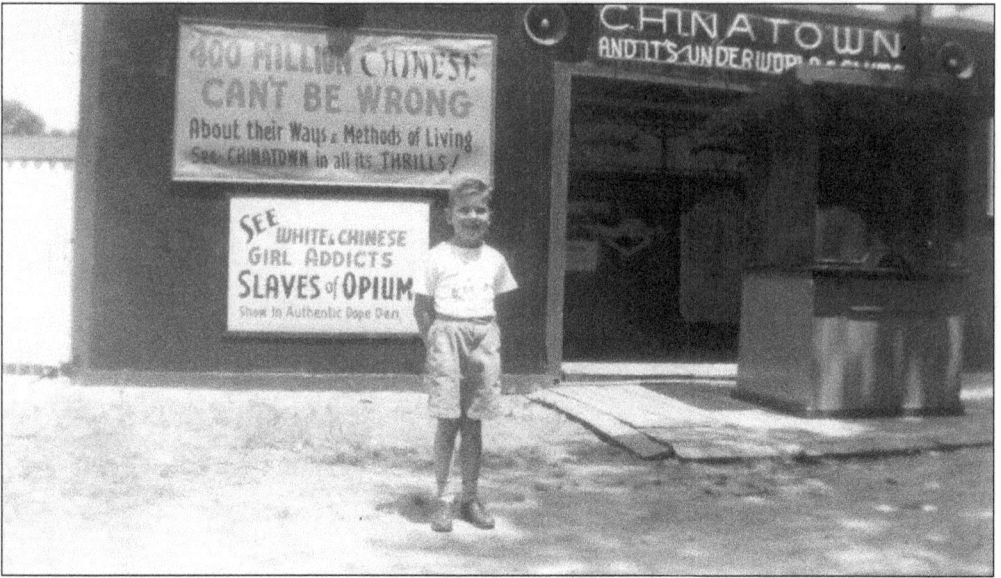

The Chinatown wax museum was designed to attract patrons by presenting topics that were still considered "forbidden" during the 1950s. Depicting the Asian sectors of large cities, Chinatown presented dimly lit scenes that portrayed opium dens inhabited by both white and Chinese girls who had become opium addicts. (Larry Wasserman Collection.)

Cedar Point's talented public relations director, Bill Evans, was instrumental in bringing a string of free acts to the resort during the 1950s. These acts included aerial acts, wirewalkers, and unicyclists who performed on spiraling towers. (Larry Wasserman Collection.)

While new rides, funhouses, and exhibits appeared on the Cedar Point midway, many of the old standards remained. The Tumble Bug, a perennial favorite with resort visitors, was given a facelift and a new neon sign.

Another old midway favorite was the Rocket Ship ride owned by veteran concessionaire Al Tedaldi. The Circle Swing ride originally operated with airplane cars, but shiny stainless steel rocket cars were introduced during the 1930s. The Honeymoon Express dark ride is located to the right of the rocket car.

Albert J. Tedaldi, who owned the Rocket Ship ride and the Loop-O-Plane, was also the proprietor of the Laff-in-the-Dark. Tedaldi purchased many of the rides previously owned by Roy Parker's Concourse Amusement Co.

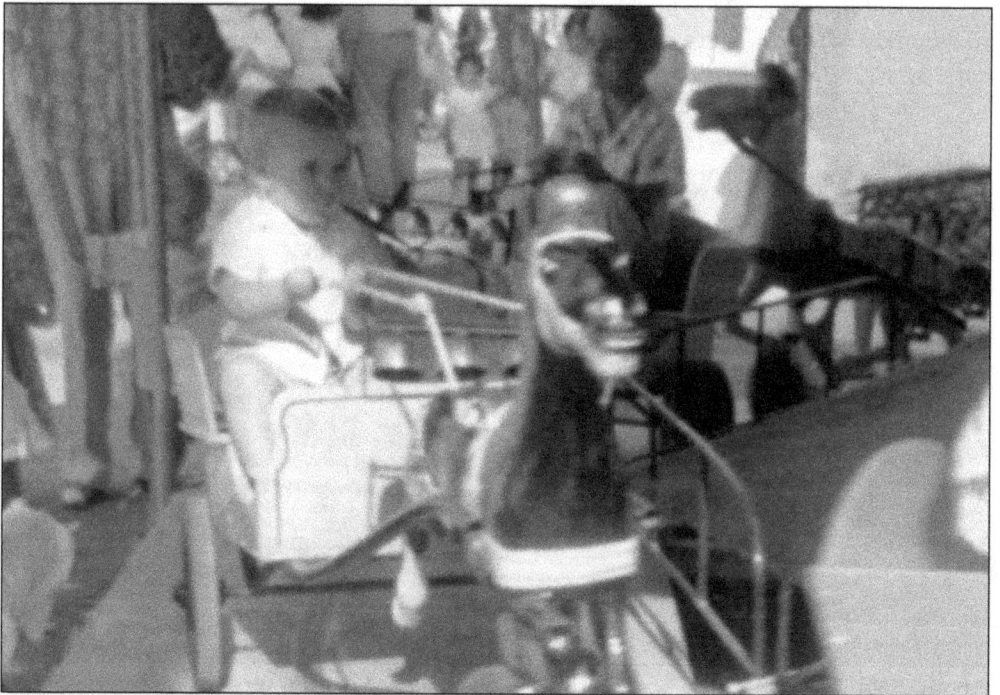

In Leonard Jefferson's Kiddieland, future Cedar Point Media Services Director Dan Feicht enjoys the pony cart ride. A few decades later, Dan became responsible for documenting and preserving Cedar Point's progress and history in photographs and video. (Cedar Point Archives.)

A 1955 view of the rejuvenated midway shows the Ferris wheel, the Rocket Ship ride, Berni's Penny Arcade, Berardi's French fry stand, and a small portion of the Concourse building. For the first time in many years, concessionaires were making money.

During the early 1900s, bathing attire was permitted only on the beach. By 1955, swim suits were a common sight almost everywhere in the resort except the restaurants and the ballroom. New rides, like the Tilt-A-Whirl, gave the old midway a modern appearance.

Unlike the midway, the employee dormitories saw little improvement during the 1950s. The men's dorms are on the right and the women's quarters on the left. The stairway led to the baths, and the open structure was used as an employee laundry area.

On the lagoons, concessionaires Joseph and Florence Santi opened a new U-Drive-'Em operation. The boats, powered by gasoline engines were especially popular with young couples and off-duty employees.

CEDAR POINT CAUSEWAY
OPENED IN 1957

In 1953, the G.A. Boeckling Co. announced plans to build a causeway to connect Cedar Point to the "mainland." The Cedar Point Causeway, intended to relieve traffic jams on the old auto road, cost $600,000 to build, but enabled the resort to handle the huge crowds that would converge on the Point in coming years. (Cedar Point Archives.)

Despite political obstacles, construction delays, and the bankruptcy of a contractor, the Cedar Point Causeway opened on June 12, 1957. The 40¢ toll immediately started repaying construction costs, and the Causeway made the resort more easily accessible.

Although the old Civil War Memorial was long gone, the beachfront was still an ideal site to honor the past. Thanks to several organizations, plaques dedicated to pioneer aviator Glenn H. Curtiss and football coach Knute Rockne were placed at the beach. Both men were part of Old Cedar Point and were destined to be remembered by New Cedar Point.

As word spread that Cedar Point was recovering, conventions and organizations again started to plan annual events at the resort. In 1958, the International Music League brought its 17th annual festival to Cedar Point.

Six

THE BIRTH OF
MODERN CEDAR POINT
1959–1970

By the early 1960s, Cedar Point was hosting 1,500,000 visitors per season. Many were amazed by the changes that had taken place in a few short years. A new concrete midway, anchored at the center by the Coliseum, included new designs, floral displays, and a miniature golf course. (Cedar Point Archives.)

When the rebirth of Cedar Point began in 1959, construction manager Robert McKay erected a sign that declared, "This Park is Under Construction, and Always Will Be." Since that day, expansion and construction at Cedar Point has never ceased.

ALLAN HERSCHELL
1865 MINIATURE TRAIN
MIDWAY – ABOUT 1960

One of the first new rides installed was an "1865" miniature frontier train. The "1865" was built by the Allan Herschell Co. of North Tonawanda, New York, one of the world's leading builders of carousels and other amusement rides. (Cedar Point Archives.)

The Monorail, envisioned as a futuristic form of urban transit, was first installed at Akron's Summit Beach Park in 1957. When Summit Beach closed at the end of the 1958 season, the Monorail was moved to Cedar Point by its builder, the Ohio Mechanical Handling Co.

The Monorail quietly negotiated a three-quarter mile track that took passengers almost to the edge of the bay. In 1959, the Monorail generated more income than any other ride on the new midway.

The Scamper, a small roller coaster of the Wild Mouse variety, was erected at the far end of the new concrete midway, not far from the lagoons. The Scamper was the first roller coaster built at Cedar Point since 1929. (Larry Wasserman Collection.)

An entire section of the new Cedar Point was designed on an Old West theme. In addition to the "1865" train, the park operated a live mule train and a Western stage coach. Because of their low rider capacity and increasing crowds, these attractions only lasted a few seasons. (Cedar Point Archives.)

Until a new games building could be constructed, new or refurbished games were housed in the renovated Concourse building. In addition, portable games in trailers were temporarily located throughout the midway. (Larry Wasserman Collection.)

A temporary attraction was the German-built funhouse, the Hofbrau Haus. Temporary rides and games permitted the management to expand the midway until larger and more spectacular permanent attractions could be installed. (Larry Wasserman Collection.)

117

The Satellite Jr. was considered a spectacular ride when it operated at the center of the new midway during the early 1960s. Unfortunately, the ride arrived at Cedar Point without detailed instructions, and the park's staff was faced with a giant jigsaw puzzle to solve during assembly.

A major undertaking by Cedar Point, Inc. was the construction of a large marina on the bay side of the Peninsula. Originally constructed with just 250 dock spaces, by 1967, it was expanded to handle 750 boats and was considered one of the finest marinas on the Great Lakes.

A section of the new funway included a Dodgem ride (left), a Rifle Range, and a steel-tracked Wild Mouse roller coaster. In the foreground is one of the floral displays that became a hallmark of the new Cedar Point. (Larry Wasserman Collection.)

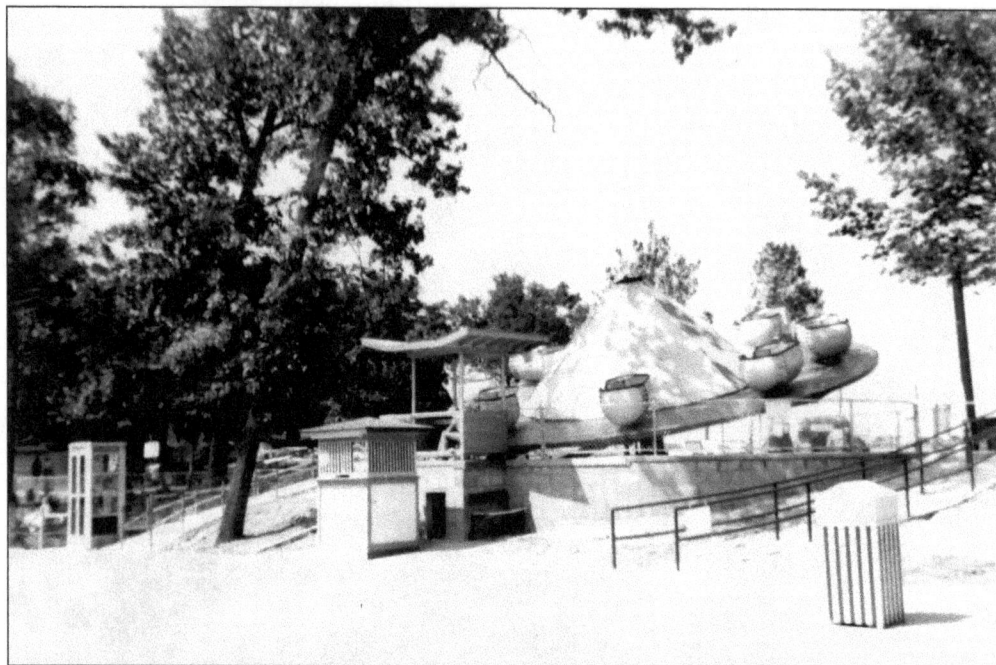

Invented in 1931, by L. Luzern Custer, the Bubble Bounce was not a new concept in riding devices. Its three-way motion, however, made it a popular ride in the early 1960s. Within a few years, it was replaced by more modern and exciting rides. (Larry Wasserman Collection.)

The E-Z-Go Taxi was an early attempt by the new management to find a convenient method of transporting visitors around the ever-expanding midway. The driver-hostess, attired in a white dress adorned with the park's new logo, also served as a good will ambassador and information service.

The Rotor arrived on the midway in time for the 1961 season. A ride that used centrifugal force to hold riders against a floorless wall, the Rotor was created by German inventor Ernst Hoffmeister in 1948. It did not gain popularity in the United States, however, until marketed by the Velare Brothers during the 1950s and 1960s. (Larry Wasserman Collection.)

George Roose's wife, Ellie, converted one of the old Pagoda buildings into the new resort's first major souvenir pavilion. The Pagodas were built during George Boeckling's reign and originally housed the Cedar Point post office, rental lockers, and restrooms. (Larry Wasserman Collection.)

The Antique Cadillac Car ride and the Turnpike ride were installed during the early 1960s, and both have remained popular attractions for more than 40 years. Unlike most midway rides, they offer a degree of rider control and participation.

Although the Sky Wheel was originally developed during the 1930s, the Allan Herschell Co. began manufacturing an improved version in 1960, and Cedar Point was one of the first parks to install this towering double Ferris wheel.

Cedar Point's new managers were quick to utilize the old lagoons. The Western Cruise boats were designed especially for the shallow lagoons, and riders were treated to animated scenes of animals, pioneer settlers, and hostile Indians. The first boat was built in the Cedar Point shops, where parts of old Hotel Breakers bedsteads were used to create decorations.

Under George Roose's direction, Hotel Breakers received a new entrance façade. The hotel was completely repainted, and a plan to modernize rooms was undertaken. Private baths were installed in many rooms, a coffee shop was opened and the lobby was extensively refurbished.

Cedar Point, Inc. continued operating the bay ferries, transporting park visitors and employees alike across the bay. Here the *Cedar Point II*, G.A. *Boeckling II*, and *Cedar Point* are shown being winterized. Note the cast iron streetlamps from Old Cedar Point.

Public Relations Director Bill Evans introduced a massed band program for opening day of the 1962 season. Inviting bands from all over the region, Evans' program produced volumes of publicity and was the envy of the amusement industry. In 1967, the event attracted 8,300 musicians from 105 high school bands.

124

George Roose and a group of investors formed the Cedar Point & Lake Erie Railroad and constructed a complete narrow gauge railway. Antique, coal-burning engines were restored, passenger coaches were built, and 6,000 cubic yards of earth was moved to create a roadbed.

The Cedar Point & Lake Erie Railroad opened with two steam locomotives in 1963. Five years later, the line operated six locomotives and carried 1,500,000 passengers during the summer season. The station was moved several times to accommodate midway expansions. (Larry Wasserman Collection.)

The Mill Race was only the second flume ride of its kind built in the United States. Debuting in 1963, the Mill cost $300,000, was 1,230 feet long, and sent boats splashing down a 28-foot hill.

The Blue Streak was the first major wooden roller coaster constructed at Cedar Point since the 1929 Cyclone. Designed and built by veteran coaster engineer Frank Hoover in 1964, the Blue Streak is 72 feet high and 2,400 feet long. Equipped with Philadelphia Toboggan Co. trains, the high ride required 200,000 board feet of lumber and rests on 559 concrete footers.

126

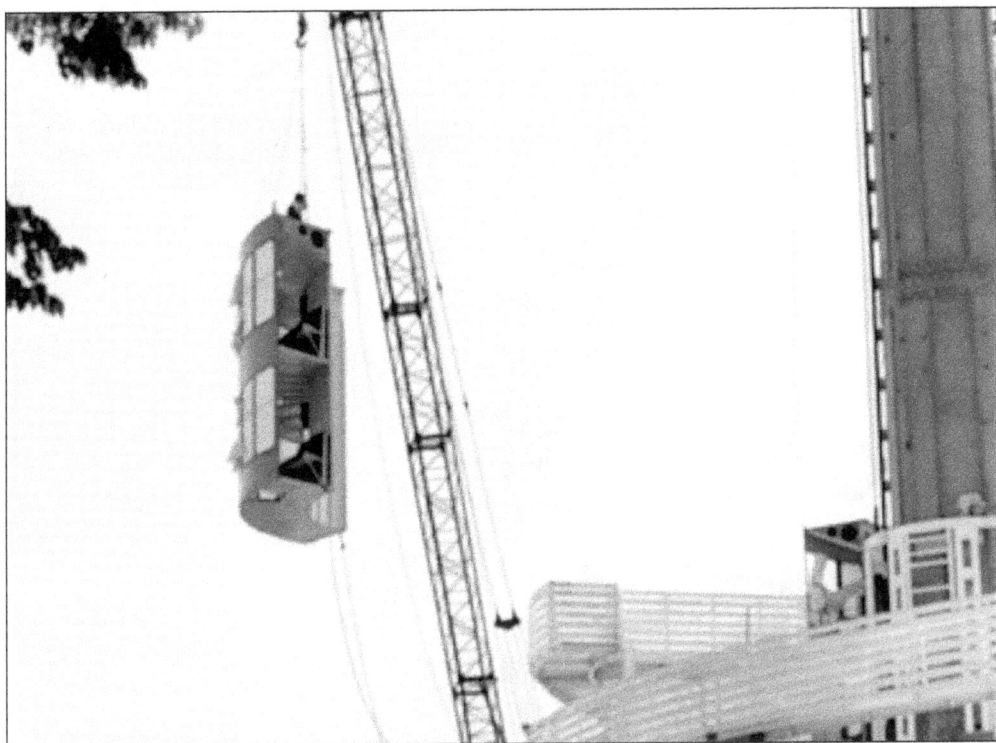

The year after the Blue Streak opened, the Space Spiral was constructed near the lake. The 330-foot tower supported a 60-passenger revolving capsule that carried riders 200 feet above the midway for a spectacular view of the park and Lake Erie.

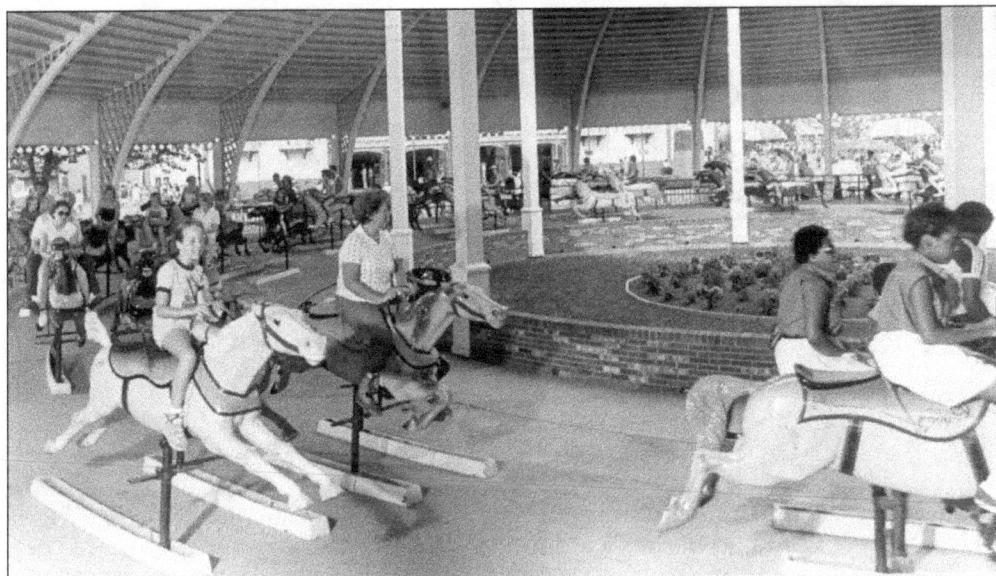

The American Racing Derby was built by Prior and Church of Venice, California, in 1921. It was originally installed at Cleveland's Euclid Beach Park, where it operated through the 1965 season. The following year, the simulated horse-race ride, renamed Cedar Downs, became an important and historical part of the Cedar Point midway. (Cedar Point Archives.)

The Pirate Ride was originally designed for Freedomland, an unsuccessful theme park located outside of New York City. When Freedomland closed, the Pirate Ride was moved to Cedar Point for the 1966 season. Passengers cruised in miniature pirate ships along the channels past scenes of pirate life and sea battles.

Cedar Point's rebirth during the 1960s was just the beginning. The park has grown bigger and better each year for more than four decades. So much so that it has been named "Best Amusement Park in the World" by 21st century trade publications. Attendance skyrocketed from 970,000 in 1959 to 2,555,000 in 1967. In 1969, Cedar Point rides carried 31,427,408 passengers in a little over 100 days. On the financial side, revenues skyrocketed from $1,338,807 in 1959 to $18,000,000 ten years later. All of this was just a preview of things to come at "The Roller Coaster Capital of the World."

Visit us at
arcadiapublishing.com

www.ingramcontent.com/pod-product-compliance
Lightning Source LLC
Chambersburg PA
CBHW080852100426
42812CB00007B/2005